Illustrations credits:

Archivio White Star/Marcello Bertinetti:
Cover, back-cover pp. 2-3, 8, 10-11, 12, 19, 21,
23, 29, 32-33, 35, 36, 39, 44-45 47, 59, 76-77,
81, 86-87, 88, 90-91, 92, 94-95.
Archivio White Star/Carlo De Fabianis:
pp. 9, 18, 22, 24, 31, 37, 38, 40, 48, 51, 58, 61,
69,
Archivio White Star/Angela White:
pp. 6, 15, 20, 25, 30, 34, 41, 46, 50, 53, 54-55,
65, 74, 78, 85, 89.
A. Bardi/Panda Photo:
p. 13.
Giuliano Colliva:
pp. 14, 42, 49, 83.
Damm/Zefa:
p. 60.
Cesare Gerolimetto:
pp. 26, 27, 28, 43, 57, 62, 64, 66, 70, 75, 82.
R. Kord/Zefa:
p. 93.
Mazzeschi/Focus Team:
p. 52.
Norman/Zefa:
p. 4.
A. Petretti/Panda Photo:
p. 71
P. Sclarandis/Sie:
p. 67.
Starphoto/Zefa:
pp. 72-73.
Angelo Tondini/Focus Team:
pp. 7, 56, 63, 68, 84.

Printed and bound in Singapore.

First published in English in 1991 by Tiger
Books International PLC, London.

This 1991 edition published by
Crescent Books, distributed by
Outlet Book Company, Inc.
A Random House Company
225 Park Avenue South
New York
New York 10003

ISBN 0-517-05877-4
87654321

INSIDE
LONDON

TEXT
SIMONA TARCHETTI

DESIGN
PATRIZIA BALOCCO

CRESCENT BOOKS
New York

With no time to look or listen, the river, accompanied by the smell of rain in the air, leaves the old seat of Scotland Yard on one side and slips under the arched bridges. By the grim Tower of London, it has buried and abandoned any vestige of beauty; on the seaward side, this course of water becomes a tireless worker and "sweats oil and tar" (T.S. Eliot) until, after abandoning the numerous bulkheads of the India and Jamaica Docks, it opens out yieldingly to the North Sea. The Thames, the liquid history of London, has been the main road on which English prosperity was built. This rather unattractive scenario of wharves, silos and barges accompanied by the constant hum of steamers, forms a backdrop to the glorious parliament building which vibrates with the chimes of Big Ben and to the elegant Tower Bridge with its unmistakable, twin-towered profile.

All of London is contained in this portait: a European metropolis, materially isolated from the continent, but spiritually impregnated with an effervescent human vitality, that invariably defies all the superficial and sometimes gratuitous attempts which historians, writers, journalists and sociologists have made to define the urban character of London.

Officially, the capital of the United Kingdom and of the Commonwealth, and cradle of the most widely-spoken language in the world, the City of London extends for a few hectares around Tower Bridge. This so-called "square mile" has never grown since the Middle Ages: indeed, the City, seat of centuries-old insurance companies and modern management offices of Japanese companies, is the least inhabited part of any European metropolis. The disorderly ensemble of villages and districts which gravitate around it is known as Greater London, which extends its tentacles for hundreds of square miles along the Thames and the surrounding countryside and is home to more than 9 million people. Since 1986, London has been governed by its 33 or so local councils. Every borough has its own individuality, dictated by the personality of its inhabitants and by a rhythm of life which marks its character. It is difficult to explain the perplexity and astonishment one feels when faced with the unpredictable and contrasting facets of this capital in which, alongside ineffable English customs, there are so many areas, each different from the next, with an extremely heterogeneous and multi-racial urban population.

Today, the City still preserves something of its medieval style, despite the reconstruction which has taken place in the post-war period and the encroachment of modern skyscrapers. The economic capital of the country, where the dominion of the audacious mercantile bourgeoisie and then of the powerful modern-day businessmen permitted the introduction and the development of economic and social democracy in the heart of England and the world, extends from Fleet Street, the original home of the press agencies and national newspapers, to the old Stock Exchange and on to the headquarters of the prestigious Bank of England.

The political capital is to be found at Westminster, which for centuries has been the residence of the monarchy and the parliamentary institutions. Today, this area is famous for its monuments: Westminster Abbey, where the English sovereigns

are crowned, was built at the beginning of the tenth century on the site of an old Saxon church but was completely rebuilt and changed artistically in successive epochs; a little further away, still on the left bank of the Thames, is the imposing Parliament building with its fanciful, audacious Gothic style. It is decorated with spires, whose reflections stretch out over the river in the light of the setting sun, further highlighting its unmistakable profile. Beside it rises up the majestic clock tower, symbol of English punctuality and a world-famous monument for the precision of its time signal, despite the fact that the clock mechanism is still wound up by hand. To the chimes of Big Ben which accompany the changing of the seasons, London replies with alacrity, dressing herself in new and continuous variations of light; sometimes diffuse and alluring, as on a warm summer's evening, sometimes touching and melancholy in the thick November fog, sometimes bright and exciting like a nightclub sign.

The atmosphere of this area of London remains, however, calm and extremely reserved, only the mounted sentries in front of the Horse Guards building and the "bobby" in front of 10, Downing Street revealing that this is the political heart of the capital.

8 An unmistakable and prestigious Rolls Royce. Right from the start the English company which produces these cars has offered technical perfection combined with soberly luxurious details.

9 On official occasions gentleman dress rather traditionally while the ladies show off elaborate hats.

10-11 This aerial view shows the Parliament buildings of Westminster on the left, and Lambeth Palace, seat of the Archbishop of Canterbury, in the lower right of the picture.

9

12 Whitehall leads off Parliament Square and here many ministries and Commonwealth offices are situated. Downing Street, official residence of the Prime Minister, leads off Whitehall.

13 Trafalgar Square is always full of life and is the traditional meeting place of tourists. This is the view down Whitehall.

14 Trafalgar Square, laid out by Nash in the period after 1820, is dominated by the neo-classical facade of the National Gallery and by Nelson's Column.

15 The soaring spires of the Houses of Parliament which stretch along the Thames embankment between Victoria Tower and Westminster Bridge.

16-17 The Palace of Westminster was completely rebuilt and redesigned in Gothic style by Barry and Pugin after the fire of 1834. In the foreground is Westminster Bridge.

*L*ondoners have a constant love-hate relationship with Buckingham Palace, although the ancient origins of the Royal Family's descent are unanimously recognized as a symbol of continuity and national identity.

The celebrations in Autumn for the opening of Parliament confirm the unalterable ritual value which the English royal tradition represents. Indeed, despite the effective legislative independence of the British government vis à vis the decision-making power of the crown, the presence of the Queen underlines the solemnity and the official character of the event, and every year the English render due honour to the Sovereign and renew the centuries-old oath of loyalty to the Royal Family. The atmosphere is different at the grandiose "Trooping of the Colour", a parade of flags, cavalry and musical bands on the occasion of the official celebration of the Queen's birthday. The music which accompanies the parade and the triumph of colours of the soldiers in their dress uniforms stuns the crowd of Londoners and tourists gathered together in Horse Guards Parade and all senses, including those of the heart, are tensed to capture, in the polychromatic geometries of the parade, that memory of childish dreams which, unexpectedly, seems to come to life here.

The public which gathers for other traditional sporting events is always plentiful and festive and, in England, the indelible memory of centuries of rich tradition combines with the social and international appeal of such highly professional competitions.

The charm of the national character lies in the innate and well-known contradiction between conservatism and love of the past on the one side and the dynamic hand thrust towards conquest, discovery and construction of something new on the other.

London, the most international and reserved city in the world, expresses this inconsistency in its contrasts between antique, old, modern and ultra-modern as well as in the contrasts between tourist attractions like its magnificent monuments, parks and pubs, and the indifference of the suburban areas and new satellite towns where the modern-day citizens live. Eccentric contrasts are visible at every corner of the city: on either side of Regent Street are the uninhibited quarter of Soho with its Chinese restaurants and red-light bars, and elegant Mayfair, a Georgian-style residential area with the luxurious and exclusive shops of Bond Street. Notting Hill is an area peopled by black immigrants and is a mixture of decaying and "gentrified" houses and during the Notting Hill Carnival in the month of August the streets become transformed with people in fancy dress and the rhythm of reggae music. A little further on towards Regent's Park, close to the famous Abbey Road, the residences of diplomats, pop-stars and record producers overlook the most famous cricket ground in the world (Lord's Cricket Ground).

In this complexity of character which permeates the entire life of the metropolis, eternally in equilibrium between tradition and progress, between jealously guarded "privacy" and the need for rapid and exhaustive communication, many of the best-known and striking symbols known to tourists are to be found.

20 The anachronistic, but much-loved telephone boxes can be found in the most obscure corners and small squares in the maze of London's streets.

22-23 All Londoners view the green expanses of the city parks as pleasant resting-places from which to calmly watch the light on the facades of the buildings or to enjoy a bit of fresh air on a sultry day.

24 Hyde Park is the largest green lung of the metropolis: a quite afternoon's reading is just one way of finding peace in the heart of the city.

25 In many London Parks there are special areas for practising sport in the open air; sometimes all that is needed to re-establish contact with nature is a stroll among the deer in Richmond Park.

26 Kensington Gardens, the natural continuation of Hyde Park, offers quiet corners with unspoilt lawns and woods enhanced by the statues which adorn the park.

27 Originally a hunting reserve, Regent's Park was transformed by Nash into a pleasant and luxuriant garden with weeping willows, stretches of water covered with water lilies and the splendid Queen Mary's Rose Garden.

28 In London the parks represent a precious and relaxing pause; forgetting the deafening and chaotic traffic, one can take delight in the music played by a military band.

29 A picturesque parade of the horse-drawn carts which were once used to transport beer.

*T*he streets of London are characterized by a particular means of transport which is not found in any other city: bright red buses which move slowly in the chaotic traffic, and wait, like patient animals on parade, for the lights to turn green. These double-deckers, which have made the city famous, are certainly less fast than the Underground but they enable one to savour, from the upper deck, the intricate landscape of streets, avenues and lanes which make up the complex layout of this city. No less significant are the rust-proof taxis produced in Coventry which preserve their inelegant and out-of-date form, dispensing with all false glitter in favour of the practical and the functional.

The London Underground, a network of lines which crosses the city from one end to the other, provides other surprises. The regulation of the ceaseless daily flux of sleepy workers who commute between the suburbs and the centre and of young people with weird hair styles, tourists and elegant ladies "equipped" with extravagant hats is aided by the exhaustive information about the routes on display at every stop and the system of one-way corridors which keep the crowds moving in an orderly fashion, as well as by the behavioural habits of the citizens, dictated by their strong civic sense.

On the surface, conflicting dilemmas torment the road network: the city has wide streets and handy thoroughfares which render traffic movement reasonably fluid despite the increased volume of modern-day traffic. In residential areas, on the other hand, street signs are hard to use due to the presence of many streets with the same name and because of the incongruous

way the houses are numbered in the smaller streets. Sometimes houses are known only by the extravagant, imaginative and personal names given to them by individual citizens. But in the midst of the frenzy of business and commerce, the proverbial English phlegm re-acquires vigour in the meditative solitude of St. James's Park and in the wide spaces of Hyde Park. The green areas offer a superb vantage point from which to observe the many different forms of behaviour which exist side by side in London. These range from the formality of the well-bred lady, waiting watchfully for the return of her little dog, to the disconcerting casualness of young people, and to the unexpected loquacity of Speakers' Corner in Hyde Park which is an open window on the Englishman's deep sense of democracy and acute sensitivity to freedom of thought. The quintessence of Englishness for many remains hidden in the lines of the celebrated eight columns of what used to be the first-and is now the last-page of the world famous newspaper "The Times". The cultivated reserve, so typical of British culture, was also evident in the journalistic approach of this prestigious newspaper, which, following an old custom, dedicated the first page to classified adverts instead of to the more important and academic articles. Today this national newspaper still enjoys a measure of esteem despite the fact that its layout has changed, leaving the traditional reader with a feeling of regret for that century-long typographical form.

34 Britain is a multi-cultural, multi-racial society, nevertheless one of the most imporant elements of the English character is an attachment to tradition.

35 The Mall, which leads up to Buckingham Palace, is a wide, tree-lined street in the heart of Royal London. Every day in summer, and every other day in winter, the Changing the Guard ceremony can be seen here.

36 Since 1066, every English monarch, except Edward V and Edward VIII, has been crowned in Westminster Abbey.

37 The ancient Saxon abbey, re-designed in a rich Gothic style, contains precious works of art in its side chapels; the white marble walls are enlivened with standards of cavalry regiments and by the splendid stained glass windows.

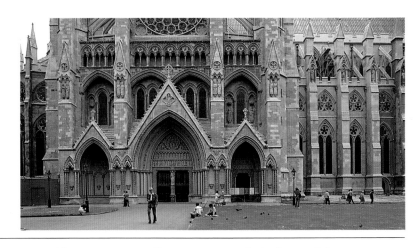

38 Over the years, Westminster Abbey underwent alterations and extensions which led to the current extraordinary mixture of architectural styles. The famous architect Sir Christopher Wren undertook restoration work and designed the West Towers.

39 The Houses of Parliament, Westminster Abbey and numerous government buildings are grouped around Parliament Square in the political heart of the capital.

*B*enjamin Disraeli, prime minister during the reign of Queen Victoria, defined London society as a "Modern Babylon", probably hinting at the teeming human activities which, despite different origins, religious beliefs and cultural backgrounds, constitute the fascinating social panorama of the metropolis.

The origins of the modern multi-racial society date back to historical events of the recent and remote past. They are the heritage of the multiple cultural influences which were superimposed one on top of the other by a series of invasions which began with the Celts a good five centuries before the birth of Christ. A constant migratory flow of people from the Asian, African and Caribbean countries which belong to the Commonwealth has added a new dimension to British culture. The British people are the amalgamation of a series of Nordic and Mediterranean races with profound Indo-European roots who have mixed more or less violently in the course of the centuries. The conquerors who poured up the Thames valley and further to the north amalgamated well with the ancient tribes who lived there, enriching their physiognomic and cultural characteristics, and initiating a process of assimilation whose slow evolution has produced today's unique and kaleidoscopic human mosaic.

The English willingly recognize that the Roman invasion marked the beginning of civilization and technology in their country. The capital itself, the ancient Londinium, was founded for strategic reasons and to this it owes the unstoppable economic and commercial development which turned it into a cultured and magnificent, cosmopolitan centre, capital of one of the most widespread empires ever to have existed. Of the splendour of the Latin civilization only fragments have been preserved and these were found more or less accidentally during building excavations: walls of Roman camps, public baths and ancient roads which led from the City to other "civitates" across the country.

With the Norman conquest, the last in the country's history, another ethnic strain was added to the already rich mixture present on the island: William I was crowned in Westminster Abbey on Christmas Day 1066, twelve months after the coronation of King Harold.

With the invasion by teutonic tribes of the British Isles at an end, the destruction which accompanied the arrival of the new rulers in the cities also ended. London, a river port protected from the fearful North Sea storms and less subject to enemy incursions, finally became the new centre of economic development, thanks to its favourable position which provided an incentive for continuous trade exchanges with other countries.

The merchants built their houses along the banks of the Thames and, for a time, the commercial centre and the magnificent government buildings became one built-up area. However, the general appearance of the city during the Middle Ages remained modest; the majority of the buildings were made of wood, urban development was spontaneous and disorganised, with winding streets and unhealthy alleys. The increase of traffic and population in successive centuries led to a horizontal, rather than vertical expansion of the city and this development

40-41 The two regiments which make up the glorious Household Cavalry can be distinguished by the different colours of their jackets and by the colour of the plumes in their hats, white for the Life Guards and red for the Blues and Royals.

mirrored the inclination of the city's inhabitants. The city expanded rapidly into the surrounding territory, swallowing up villages and outlying areas but leaving large expanses of meadow and field as if to dilute, in a bucolic greenness, the frenzied building development of the rising economic and social centre which was being consolidated.

In London the parks are the vital patches of colour which for centuries have coexisted with the city representing in a tangible manner the will of the British to maintain, even in a metropolis, a necessary reserved detachment from the international, extrovert and, occasionally, unscrupulous atmosphere which permeates all other city activities.

Some areas of London are the fruit of intelligent redevelopment which occurred after internal conflicts during the turbulent history of the English crown and the dramatic events which accompanied particular political and ecclesiastical events. All Catholic religious buildings and the monasteries were swept away when Henry VIII came to the throne and abolished all religious orders and confiscated their property.

Only some place-names remain which recall the numerous orders of monks present in the various parts of the city up to the reform of the Church of England.

London acquired many of its famous architectural masterpieces during the Stuart period, the historical period of greatest political and cultural splendour. The great English architect Inigo Jones, after visiting Italy, introduced and developed the "Palladian" style giving a touch of genial harmony to the

London panorama. Even for the English, the buildings in Covent Garden, now an animated quarter and refuge of buskers and strolling players, remain pleasantly characteristic of the Palladian style, as does the splendid Banqueting House in Whitehall which contains royal apartments with frescoes which were painted much later by Rubens.

The incessant work of embellishing royal palaces and public buildings, carried out by famous architects on behalf of aristocracy, rich bourgeoisie and the royal family itself stands in contrast with the actual dearth of historical monuments in the centre of London; that enterprising square mile which is the capital's tireless centre of vitality. The majority of the wooden buildings of the medieval city were destroyed by a terrible fire in the latter half of the 17th century, but the rapid reconstruction of the area basically followed the preceding schemes, despite the fact that a more rational town plan, based on more modern urban planning concepts was put forward. In the midst of the anonymous surrounding buildings, however, the magnificent St. Paul's Cathedral was built. This grandiose monument with its classic lines, is the seat of the Bishop of London, and is, quite rightly, considered Wren's masterpiece. It was the first building to be consecrated as a Protestant church and its beautiful cupola evokes contrasting memories of such historical events as the funeral of the illustrious politician Winston Churchill or, more recently, the magnificent celebrations for the wedding of Prince Charles and Lady Diana Spencer.

42 The headquarters of the Metropolitan Police is still known as Scotland Yard because that was the address of its first HQ, now used as a stables for police horses used in parades and normal service.

43 The streets of London daily bring out alluring contrasts between indelible tradition and modern technical progress.

44-45 From the top deck of a double-decker one certainly has a good view of the sights of London.

*T*here is an "English way" of assimilating artistic influences. Models borrowed from other European cultures are adapted to suit the function and purpose of the architectural work, exhibiting little of the Mediterranean fantasy which nonetheless represents the fertile substratum of many structural and decorative ideas. In the succession of different styles which are to be found almost everywhere, the restrained and elegant lines of the classical buildings, with their perceptibly medieval touch and the sober elegance of the royal palaces stand out.

In the 19th century, London ruled the largest empire ever to have existed and the city was transformed into a rich and refined metropolis. Beautiful dwellings in Georgian style were erected along tree-lined avenues in Mayfair, Belgravia and Kensington, which are still the most elegant and luxurious areas to live. Genuine innovations in urban planning were conceived and carried out by John Nash, King George IV's personal architect, and these can still be seen in the city centre. They include triumphal Regent Street, that wide thoroughfare for traffic, the commemorative Trafalgar Square, animated meeting place of Londoners and the frenzied roundabout of Piccadilly Circus, modern-day meeting-place of young people and tourists. In the construction of new buildings, the aristocracy and the bourgeoisie of the Victorian age used the decorative force of classical, renaissance and baroque elements, thus creating an eclectic style rich in ornament and frills, which sometimes became mannered.

The splendour of the Albert Hall and the complex of the various museums which were built to recall that golden period were in sharp contrast with the hovels of the port described by Dickens in his novels. There, thieves and cut-throats milled around the docks and the barges moored along a river made yellow by the mud stirred up by the action of the tide. With time London became a human melting pot and overcrowded city suburbs, teeming with people of every nationality, sprang up around regal Westminster, the elegant districts and the innumerable banks and administrative offices.

The technical innovations of the Industrial Revolution, with the construction of new factories and works, increased the commercial and financial dealings of London and they were accompanied, at the beginning of the century, by important social changes and a new spirit of democracy which was more solid and constructive and improved the well-being of the entire country. A surprising aspect of modern London society is the way in which the different social classes co-habit with tolerance, while still remaining extraordinarily impermeable to each other. There is an aristocratic and privileged London, a middle-class, bourgeois London and a working-class London as well as the ethnic minorities.

46 A popular area for Londoners and visitors alike is the Serpentine, an artificial lake in Hyde Park.

47 The Romans built a wooden bridge on the strategic site where Tower Bridge now stands and it was around this that ancient Londinium developed.

48 The two Gothic towers of Tower Bridge contain the machinery which lifts up the double draw-bridge to let ships past.

49 From the top of its granite column the statue of
Admiral Nelson dominates Trafalgar Square.

50 *The Yeoman Warders of the Tower of London, known as Beefeaters, were first set up by Edward VI and now constitute a charming tourist attraction.*

51 *Once the gloomy site on which capital executions were carried out, the Tower now houses collections of armour, and the fabulous crown jewels which contain the famous Koh-i-Noor diamond.*

52 Although Westminster is the real political capital of Great Britain, it has a pleasant, timeless appearance.

53 The Metropolitan Police keep a careful eye on the streets of central London.

54-55 The favourite pastimes of the British aristocracy are almost invariably connected with horses: international horse shows, thrilling polo games and fox hunting.

56 The suberb landscaping of Hyde Park with its
rich and varied planting and quiet corners makes it
a favourite spot for Londoners.

57 The Royal Botanic Gardens, called simply Kew Gardens, house exotic plants admirably mixed in with indigenous species, a Japanese pagoda and suberb glasshouses in which hundreds of splendid tropical plants are grown.

58 Famous in the 1960s, Carnaby Street is now the place in London for cheap and cheerful young fashion.

59 In Petticoat Lane there is the most incredible assortment of collectable junk: second-hand clothes, furniture and furnishings.

*A*t a first, superficial glance, London might appear vast and uniform in its stereotyped appearance, yet, it possesses a particular vitality in which two worlds, the cosmopolitan and the indigenous, manage to co-exist. These two realities brush against each other everywhere, but they rarely merge. The city offers a fascinating testimony to the changes and the evolution in custom which have taken place in the last decades in the shadow of Big Ben. The impetuous vitality of youth has left its unmistakable mark, especially in the shops where tradition acts as a counterpoint to the exuberance of the new. Indeed, there are all sorts of shops in London, and if the celebrated building which is home to the legendary Harrods, most famous emporium in the city, is not sufficient to satisfy the shopping requirements of Londoners and tourists, the stalls of the flea markets in Portobello Road and Petticoat Lane will probably be able to satisfy the omnipresent connoisseur in search of original at any price.

Style and refinement distinguish the most luxurious shops for aristocratic and well-to-do Londoners: the shops of shirt-makers, shoemakers, pipe and tobacco sellers in St. James's Street and surroundings receive their noble clients with discretion in an atmosphere of exquisite, exclusive hospitality. At the other extreme, there is the continuous hubbub and the restless thronging around the latest fashions in King's Road, or the sheer variety to be found in Carnaby Street. This bustling road was made famous during the 1960s and by clothes ranging from the ultra-classical to the post-modern, from Shetland cardigans to second-hand jeans reduced to

62-63 The old, narrow Portobello Road fills up with stalls for the traditional antique market in which valuable objects are mixed with junk in a totally random fashion.

shreds, from trousers in traditional check to aggressive bomber jackets covered with studs. These and a myriad of other styles and audacious combinations, are not only on show in the windows of the shops and emporiums, but are being worn and shown off by that most singular collection of humanity which comprises the cosmopolitan crowds of London.

The indefinable attraction exerted by the presence of the most varied human customs, which here all have the same rights of citizenship, captures the attention of the visitor and directs it towards the contrasts in London. Thus, in the various rooms of Harrod's elegant Food Halls, against the backdrop of mosaics and tiles from the Victorian epoch, one can find an irresistible and incredible quantity and quality of foodstuffs of the most diverse origins, such as to satisfy "any request in any part of the world". Afternoon tea is still served according to tradition in fine china and accompanied by pastries; the classic roast beef, an institution of culinary art, must be carved according to a precise ritual, according to which only a man can carry out the delicate operation. At the other extreme, the city offers modern fast food places in Piccadilly Circus, the "take aways" and the numerous restaurants in the West End where it is possible to taste samples of the world's cuisine in luxurious and international premises. They serve exotic specialities of all sorts: African and American menus, Italian and Russian delicacies, French or Thai tit-bits, traditional Spanish and Japanese dishes in an atmosphere which is typical of the country whose specialities are being served.

*64 Berwick Street fruit and vegetable market in
the heart of Soho. The crowds that throng here are
a mixture of races from all over the world.*

65 *The busiest shops and stalls are run by the Chinese who arrived in Soho relatively recently, even though there has been a Chinese community here for at least a century.*

A typical English tradition is that of meeting friends in the local pub before heading home to the suburbs for the family meal or going on to a fashionable restaurant. "Public houses" are an essential component of British society: they represent a national institution whose origins are said to date back to Roman tabernae, which then gave way to Saxon pubs where the home produced beer was sold directly at the door in brimming beakers before the process of fermentation had finished. The atmosphere of every pub is created by its devoted clients, the habitual customers who are happy with that feeling of intimacy and pleasant sociableness, of known faces and familiar conversations which the place offers. Thus, in the heart of the city immediately after work, businessmen and journalists meet and chat about the latest events of the day. In Soho, customers come for a pint later in the evening, when the area is at its liveliest, while at corner pubs near theatres, the drink flows to refresh the actors and the public who have just come out after the shows.

According to George Orwell, the perfect pub has an indefinable atmosphere, one moment it is heated and lively because of the animated discussions which take place and the next it is calm and discreet when, after the ritual tasting of the beer, the tongue clicks, satisfied, against the palate. No room there for modern mournful plastic panels of fake mahogany and deafening music! Even today, a good pub has its walls suitably worn and blackened with time, period cobwebs are appreciated, the dartboard is an essential and the interior layout, even though extravagantly Victorian, must include comfortable corners

65 *The busiest shops and stalls are run by the Chinese who arrived in Soho relatively recently, even though there has been a Chinese community here for at least a century.*

protected by screens for the most private conversations but, at the same time, the bar where the drinks are poured must encourage socialization.

The principle attention of the publican is for the drinks and the quality of the beer and the rigid rules which must be observed in every public house. Following the best British tradition, the golden liquid must be served at room temperature and without gas. The good reputation of a pub is a result of the care and attention with which the golden fermented mixture of barley and hops is treated and stored.

Some pubs have architectural elements, a particular clientèle or a choice of furnishings and decoration which gives each pub a characteristic and unique atmosphere. All the more famous pubs, even if they they do not adorn their scarcely illuminated sign with the sought-after phrase of " the oldest English pub" boast a historical or literary connection. The tales of Dickens speak from the walls of the The Cock Tavern, while the memory of the genial intuition of a (fictitious) detective and his faithful assistant hangs in the air between the tables in the Sherlock Holmes pub, and blood-curdling contemporary articles about Jack the Ripper cover the pub of that name in the East End.

67 The iron and glass pavilions of Covent Garden were built in 1835 as a fruit and vegetable market. Now the building shown here has been converted to house shops, restaurants and cafés.

*T*he start of night-life in the metropolis helps to mitigate the sound of the pub's bell which announces the imminent ban on the sale of alcoholic drinks. Evening shadows descend along the course of the Thames and the neon signs in the squares and streets vigorously oppose the arrival of the day's end with their polychromatic palettes of vivid light. The brilliantly coloured signs outside the nightclubs give the streets of London a lively atmosphere of worldliness as the youth of the city and the visiting night-birds, who are longing to experience the metropolis, descend from Piccadilly Circus and from Oxford Street, as well as from the suburbs, in search of excitement. They loaf about between topless bars and spaghetti-houses of indescribable smells, torn between hard core pornography cinemas and exotic culinary attractions. The private clubs of Pall Mall, refined and, above all, exclusive, receive only aristocratic patrons, film stars and wealthy millionaires. In the elegant atmosphere of the club, barons, counts, lords and ladies, offspring of royal loins and top models chat, comfortably seated in plush surroundings, about the most recent political happenings. The garish and modern discotheques which stretch from the West End to the King's Road and Kensington offer hospitality to the latest trends of the New Romantic fashion, to those who follow the lifestyle of the West Coast, and host revivals of 1970s funk shows in an electrifying atmosphere of psychedelic lights and video clips. In each discotheque we can count on the unfailing presence of numerous groups of tourists, recording stars, striptease artistes, punks and many other miscellaneous groups.

69 There is an unrivalled range of things to do in the evenings and one can go to the theatre, to see a musical or to listen to a concert.

70 Imported from India and China and skilfully blended, tea is the favourite English drink. Fortnum and Mason is famous for its exceptional blends of tea.

71 Of all the departments in Harrods, the food-hall is certainly the most famous, both for the stunning way the food is displayed and for the mosaics.

72-73 The tourist's idea of London – raining, grey and misty!

74-75 The signs outside the pubs signal a particular and fascinating aspect of British life, made up of the atmosphere, architecture and clientèle of each pub.

74

76-77 The interior decoration of public houses make each one highly individual. A meeting place or just a place for drinking on your own, pubs have an important social role in Britain.

78 *The neon signs and the flashing advertising slogans in Piccadilly Circus at night.*

79 *In Knightsbridge 11,000 bulbs illuminate the brick-built Harrods department store.*

80 The City has a decidedly modern appearance with its numerous sky-scrapers, which were built after the war on the ruins of the area which had been destroyed by bombs during the Second World War.

81 The Royal Borough of Kensington and Chelsea is the most famous residential area for the aristocracy.

82 *The British Museum houses a fascinating collection of antiquities from all over the world. The greatest world civilizations are represented here by extraordinary and unique exhibits.*

Every evening, the cultural programme offered by the capital includes a rich and extremely varied choice of theatrical performances, concerts, opera and ballet companies. Successful plays are staged in the major West End theatres while, in the suburbs and smaller theatres, the stages are animated with "alternative" avant-garde theatrical productions or situation comedies full of humour and strikingly good ideas. The perennial ferment of the London music scene leads us to the effervescent heart of this world capital of sound, where the impeccable musical performances of the London Symphony Orchestra, under the baton of prestigious conductors, alternate with more intimate concerts of chamber music. The massive gatherings at Wembley stadium, stage and barometer of international rock music, stand in contrast to the most exotic and composed rhythms and melodies which emerge from a still fertile musical humus made up of pop stars, impresarios, talent scouts, shabby rock bands and radical jazz clubs.

From the times of "swinging London", the different expressions of pop music have involved and shaken society, dividing young people into Mods and Rockers, Punks and Skinheads, Hell's Angels and Dandies. London is a lavish display cabinet for every new adolescent cult which emerges with disconcerting vitality from the conformism of adult society. From here, various youthful lifestyles, scathing and subversive at first, then acceptable and inoffensive, spread out over the continent and on the other side of the Atlantic, creating myths and multiple disguises with which even today millions of young people identify.

But the evolution of mass culture finds its deepest and most vital roots, as well as its mirror, in the sound of the Beatles and in the provocative words of the songs of the Rolling Stones and the Sex Pistols. If Wembley Stadium once represented the temple of non-conformity and youth protest for the flower people and the wild fans of rock in a land where traditions were firmly rooted, for the youth of today it represents a traditional meeting place from which to launch messages, at times of accusation and at times of solidarity, to the world. London society is pervaded by so many discordant aspects, which are often intangible but rarely without influence.

Despite all the modern customs and attitudes, the history and the centuries-old traditions sustain that unshakable faith which the British people have in their own strength, enabling them to continue to grow and build modern urban society. The obvious contrast between tradition and the permissiveness of modern-day living make London a unique city, suitable for any human fantasy or mood, but reluctant to accept narrow definitions or the simplistic impressions which an unwise visitor might receive from this complicated cosmopolitan city.

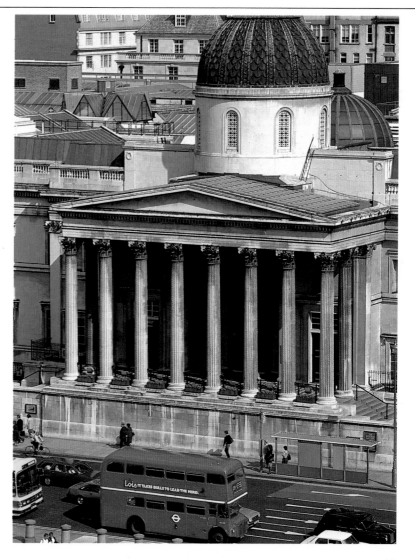

83 The National Gallery is one of the most famous art galleries in the world and its collection includes valuable masterpieces by the most important European artists.

84 Knightsbridge is renowned for its luxury shops and prestigious hotels.

85 Royal events and ceremonies are an integral part of city life.

86-87 The splendid ceremony of "Trooping the Colour" dates back to 1805 and celebrates the official birthday of the Queen on the Saturday nearest to 11th June. During the military parade, the royal horse and foot guards are inspected by Her Majesty who wears dress uniform.

88-89 During the official ceremony, the crowd watches silently, aware that they are witnessing one of the most spectacular events in the Royal calendar.

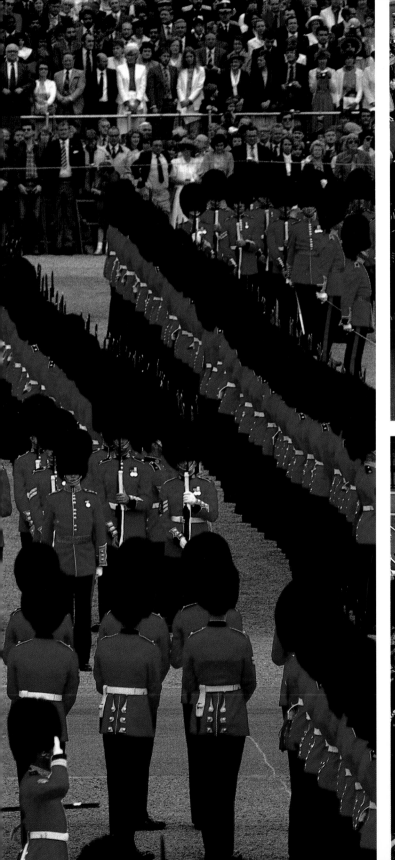

90-91 *At dusk, the silhouettes of the buildings around Trafalgar Square made a dramatic picture.*

91

92 In the evening light London takes on a fascinating and seductive atmosphere.

93 *Big Ben is famous for the accuracy of its signal and for the sound of its famous bell.*

94-95 *A contemporary view of the City with Wren's masterpiece, St. Paul's Cathedral, squashed between modern buildings and sky-scrapers.*